EXPLORING
THE
UNITED KINGDOM

WRITTEN BY
NOAH LEATHERLAND

LET'S GO TO... **WALES**

AF192521

BookLife
PUBLISHING

©This edition published in 2026.
First published in 2024.
BookLife Publishing Ltd.
King's Lynn, Norfolk
PE30 2HN, UK

A catalogue record for this book is available from the British Library.

ISBN: 978-1-80505-613-3

Written by:
Noah Leatherland

Edited by:
Elise Carraway

Designed by:
Amelia Harris

FSC
www.fsc.org
MIX
Paper | Supporting responsible forestry
FSC® C011748

Image Credits

All images are courtesy of Shutterstock.com, unless otherwise specified. With thanks to Getty Images, Thinkstock Photo and iStockphoto.
Recurring – Stephen Rees, Ton Photographer 4289, olgers. Cover – naulicrea, SLdesign, 2d collection, andrew mappouras, Fanfo, Marina Kryukova, Martina Hardiman, NPavelN, Volodymyr Voronov. 2–3 – Billy Stock. 4–5 – VectorShop, Renny Oktarianti, steve estvanik, Art Gallery of South Australia, Public domain via Wikimedia Commons. 6–7 – steved_np3, Billy Stock, Matagonca, vectortatu. 8–9 – Valerie2000, Edd Mitchell. 10–11 – Billy Stock, Richard Whitcombe, BBA Photography, Alfmaler. 12–13 – Nina Alizada, threerocksimages. 14–15 – New Africa, SLdesign, Brent Hofacker. 16–17 – Alistair Scott, Pierre de la Mare, Art-is-Power. 18–19 – Marco Iacobucci Epp, marcokenya, Ink Drop. 20–21 – Nacho Mena, Dave scar, Buch and Bee. 22–23 – Lukasz Pajor, Tomas Marek, artdock.

CONTENTS

WORDS THAT LOOK LIKE THIS CAN BE FOUND IN THE GLOSSARY ON PAGE 24.

WELCOME TO THE UNITED KINGDOM

The United Kingdom is made up of four countries – England, Scotland, Wales and Northern Ireland. Although they might look small on a map, these countries have so much to explore.

SCOTLAND

ENGLAND

NORTHERN IRELAND

WALES

WALES

Wales and England were the first countries in the United Kingdom to join together. In 1536, King Henry VIII made it so that England and Wales were ruled by the same laws.

KING HENRY VIII

WALES ALSO HAS ITS OWN GOVERNMENT THAT MAKES ITS OWN DECISIONS.

CARDIFF

Cardiff is the capital city of Wales. A capital city is usually the most important city in the country. At one point, Cardiff was shipping more coal around the world than any other city.

COAL WAS VERY IMPORTANT TO LOTS OF COUNTRIES.

Cardiff Castle sits near the centre of the city. The castle has been there for hundreds of years. Different parts have been built as different people have ruled it.

THE NORMAN KEEP INSIDE CARDIFF CASTLE

SNOWDONIA

Snowdonia is one of the most visited places in the United Kingdom. Snowdonia is an area with lots of <u>natural</u> beauty. Mount Snowdon is the most popular sight there.

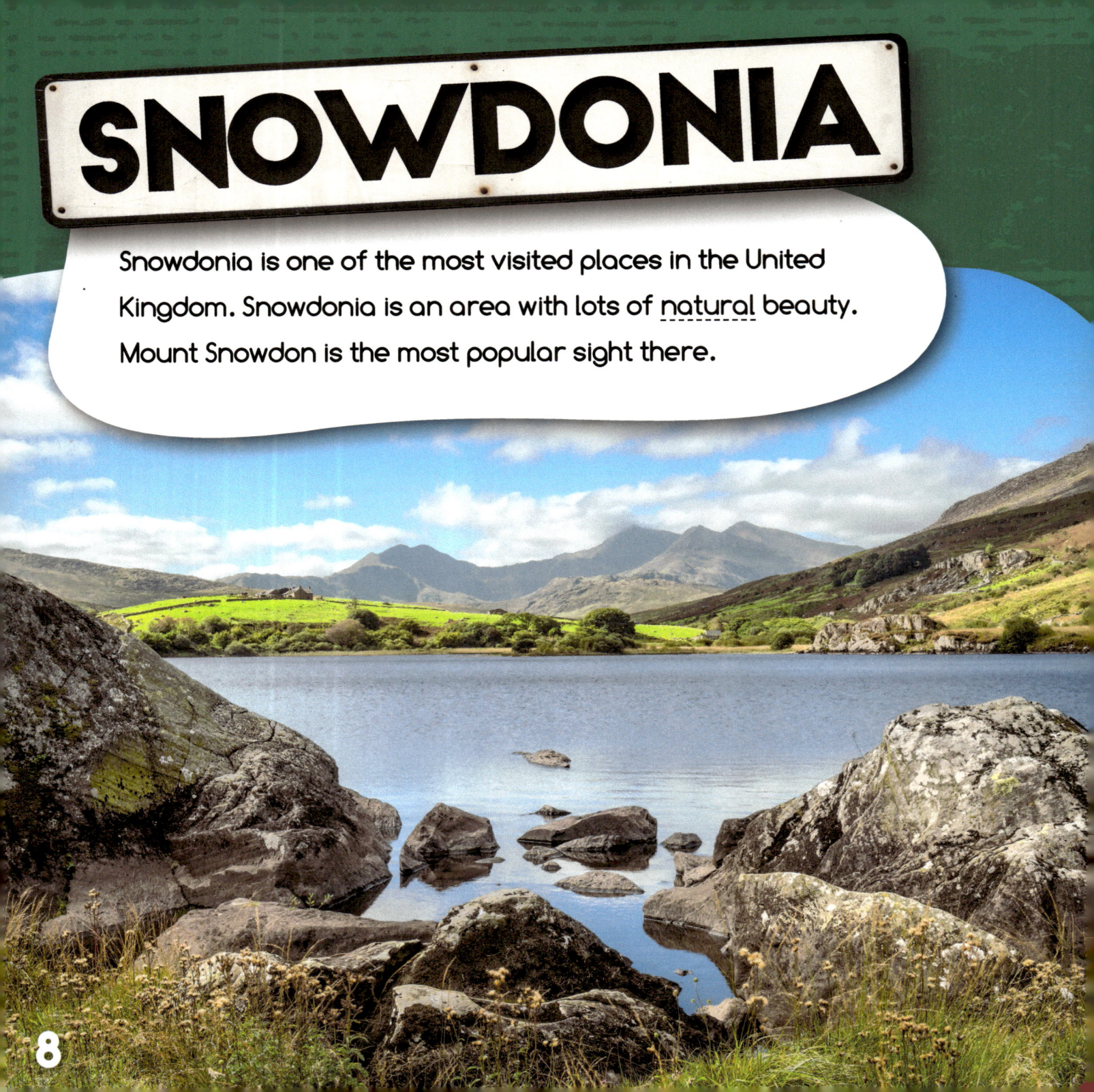

Mount Snowdon is the highest mountain in Wales. It reaches over 1,000 metres above the sea. Mount Snowdon is so big that it can often be seen from Ireland on a clear day!

SIGHTS TO SEE

Caerphilly Castle is the largest castle in Wales. It was built in the 1200s to be a strong defence. Caerphilly Castle has tall walls, big towers and a huge <u>moat</u> around it.

MOAT

Wales is famous for its beautiful <u>coastline</u>. Skomer Island is one of the most famous Welsh islands. It is home to lots of amazing animals, such as puffins and razorbills.

PUFFIN

RAZORBILL

WELSH RAREBIT

Welsh rarebit is a <u>traditional</u> dish that has been eaten in Wales since the 1500s. Some historians believe that Welsh rarebit got its name as a joke to make fun of dishes with fancy names.

The first part of making Welsh rarebit is the sauce. A thick cheese sauce is made by melting cheese and mixing it with other <u>ingredients</u>. Then, it gets poured over toasted bread.

DAFFODILS AND LEEKS

The daffodil is the national flower of Wales. Daffodils grow around St David's Day, the Welsh national day of celebration. Their yellow petals are said to be a symbol of hope and new beginnings.

The leek is a vegetable that is also a symbol of Wales. One <u>legend</u> says that many years ago, a Welsh leader told his soldiers to wear a leek on their armour like a badge.

THE WELSH DRAGON

Although it is not a real creature, the national animal of Wales is the red dragon. The dragon is such a big symbol of Wales that it is on the Welsh flag.

A STATUE OF THE RED DRAGON AT CARDIFF CASTLE

A red dragon has been used as a symbol of Wales for hundreds of years. One legend says that the red dragon keeps Wales safe by fighting off a white dragon.

RUGBY

Rugby is one of the most popular sports in Wales. It has been bringing the Welsh people together for many years. There are over 300 rugby clubs in the country.

In rugby, points are scored when the ball is placed on the ground past the other team's goal line. Kicking the ball between the other team's goal posts is another way to score points.

SCORING POINTS BY PLACING THE BALL IS CALLED GETTING A TRY.

LOVE SPOONS

Love spoons are traditional Welsh gifts that date back hundreds of years. A love spoon is a wooden spoon that is cut by hand. They can be cut into all kinds of shapes.

Love spoons are given as gifts. Traditionally, they were given as gifts between two people hoping to fall in love. Today, they are given to all sorts of loved ones for different celebrations.

EXPLORING THE UNITED KINGDOM

There is so much more about Wales that you have yet to explore. There are so many places to see and interesting traditions to learn about.

LLANDDWYN ISLAND

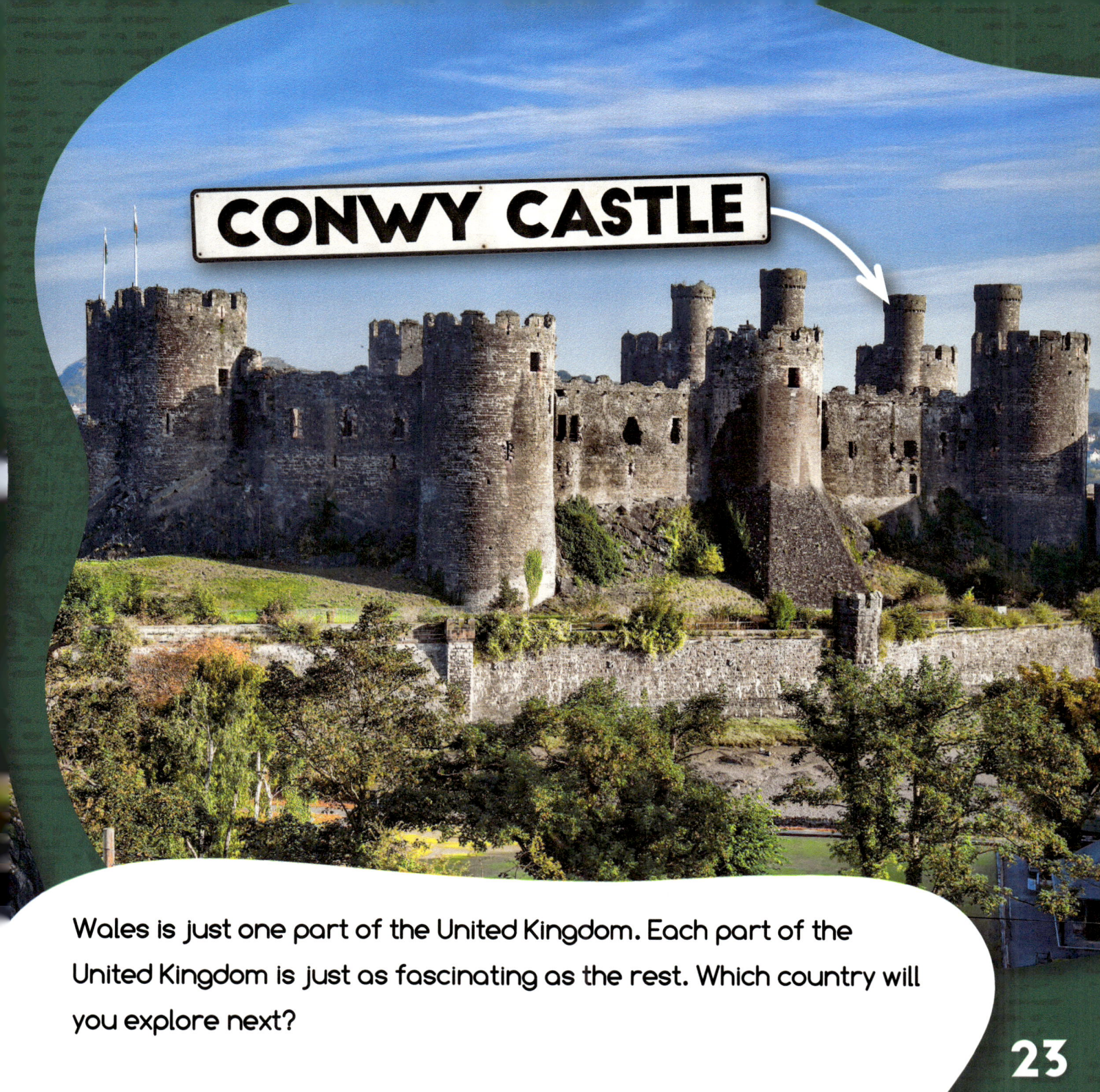

CONWY CASTLE

Wales is just one part of the United Kingdom. Each part of the United Kingdom is just as fascinating as the rest. Which country will you explore next?

GLOSSARY

COASTLINE	the area where the land meets the sea
GOVERNMENT	a group of people with the power to run a country
INGREDIENTS	the different foods that are combined to make a dish
LAWS	rules that a group of people must follow
LEGEND	an old story that may or may not be true
MOAT	water around a castle that keeps people out
NATIONAL	to do with things that are shared by people in a country
NATURAL	found in nature and not made by people
SYMBOL	a thing that is used as a sign of something else
TRADITIONAL	to do with beliefs, customs or ways of behaving that have been around for a long time

INDEX